Mental Health Therapy Through Public Comment

By Daniel K. Arnold

Acknowledgments:

Special thanks to Aleshia Echols, CMHA-CEI Executive Assistant for challenging me to preserve all my Board of Directors Public Comments since 2016.

Thanks to all the attentive leaders who have listened to me and gave me feedback at Community Mental Health Authority of Clinton, Eaton, and Ingham Counties.

And… Number One thank you to God from which my inspiration comes!

Mental Health Therapy Through Public Comment

By Daniel K. Arnold

Chapter 1 – Introduction

I have not always been at peace with a mental health diagnosis. Years have gone by with weight gain, hard-core fatigue and other side effects of psychotropic drugs. I wince at old pictures of a person who looked very medicated. Many times I have resented that first visit to a mental hospital in 1999. Every experience has become my story. I have learned to embrace trials and difficulty as learning opportunities to see the world for what it really is in order to report on it.

Much progress has been made in my health journey. More productivity is still to be achieved. I know that I am thankful for life and people are noticing.

Early on, I believed that the mental health system was corrupt. I bucked my therapy and condition. I was convinced that I had achieved a healing level that needed no more meds. I fell on my face again and again. Some faith leaders encouraged me to put my faith in miracle healing. They taught that medication is translated as "pharmakeia" and that an earlier translation version of the Bible likened this medication to evil sorcery. I bought in hook, line and sinker eager to escape the side effects of prescription drugs.

Some of my adventures off medication resulted in a brief period of extreme productivity and weight loss. Many people seemed to encourage this hypomanic stage. However, when the inevitable crash came, I felt abandoned and misunderstood.

I have been resisting the system of mental health for almost 20 years until recently. Today, on a minimum dosage of medication, I see myself as special, not an accident or illness. I know that God has created me in this way like the rapper Kanye West who said, "I'm not Bipolar. I'm a Super Hero."

Revelation! And revelation has come with this amazing journey of pain, discovery, and freedom. I was not always feeling this level of blessing, but I have never given up on pursuing a life of meaning.

The following CMHA-CEI Board of Directors Public Comment Speeches span from November 17th 2016 to Present. They

show me as someone who copes with pain

by writing and presenting: Mental Health

Therapy Through Public Comment. Enjoy

this adventure with me!

Mental Health Therapy Through Public

Comment

By Daniel K. Arnold

Thursday, November 17, 2016

<u>Board of Directors CEI-CMHA Speech</u>

Thank you for the opportunity to speak to you. I am Daniel Arnold, a self-appointed Rights Advocate for Mental Health.

I spend the majority of my time, six days a week, serving and enjoying the Non-Profit, Justice in Mental Health Organization, also known as JIMHO.

This Non-Profit is essential to our community. It is the last stomping ground for many hurting people. It is more than a resting place, but a center where people are nourished, have a chance to grow, and are supported by peers.

At times, JIMHO has been virtually my only non-judgmental support. Empathy is the key at this center that badly needs your support.

JIMHO is a peer support model for about sixty mental health drop-ins around the state of MI.

What happens here must be celebrated!

Care about us. Care about our needs.

Thank you for your time and consideration.

Mental Health Therapy Through Public

Comment

By Daniel K. Arnold

Chapter 3 – Advocate

My first documented speech at

CMHA-CEI Board of Directors was

succinct. I found a great deal of support

from the building Justice in Mental Health

Organization Drop-In and still do. At the

time, I was discovering dignity in journalism

and my new consumer advisory council

positions. I saw myself as an "advocate,"

not as a messed up person. Yes, I had been

hospitalized repeatedly as a broken record,

but I had spirit and life.

JIMHO was an important place for me

to thrive at the time. Although I spend less

time there now, I appreciate a place where I

do not feel judged as disabled among peers

and can build relationships. I recruited

many writers from this pool and would

invite guest speakers to do open forums in

the building.

Mental Health Therapy Through Public

Comment

By Daniel K. Arnold

Chapter 4 – Speech #2

Community Mental Health Authority of

Clinton, Eaton and Ingham Counties

Board of Directors Meeting:

Daniel Arnold, Public Comment

"Status of Mental Health Services Lansing,

MI, USA, End of the Year 2017."

Thursday, December 21, 2017, 6:00pm.

To Whom it May Concern:

Hi, My name is Daniel Arnold & I will be

giving you my report on the status of Mental

Health Services in Greater Lansing.

I am a Child & Mental Health Advocate

who works for _______ Preschool. I serve on

two mental health consumer advisory

councils. I speak at local & state

conferences on mental health. I am an

author and avid in my community.

This is my year end summary:

There are many services being provided to

the community with the indirect or direct

help of CMHA-CEI.

Thankfully, mental health consumers who do not feel they belong have a place to go this holiday season.

Justice in Mental Health Organization has their celebration as usual reaching many needy consumers. People who struggle with mental illness, addictions, and homelessness are all able to come if they receive services from CMH.

This is a necessary tremendous sacrifice for peer support specialists to give up their holiday season to serve the broken community. Thankfully, people have a place to go.

Charter House Clubhouse will also be having a holiday celebration thankful to the hardworking CMHA-CEI Staff that treat consumers with respect and dignity.

Charter House is a place where people can feel inspired to be the best that they can be. There is no judgment and great motivation to move forward in preparation for work.

The Clubhouse Model is very important and international. There is a local, state, national, and international model that supports one another.

Right now, Charter House is leading the state in modeling advocacy for an important issue. Lakeshore Clubhouse in Holland, MI faces a threat of closing down due to lack of funding from Ottawa County CMH.

Charter House and other clubhouses around the state are lobbying for the protection of this important resource.

Consumers feel empowered and have a voice at Charter House. We are working together to write board members, politicians, and media. We are making a difference!

JIMHO is also a model mental health service for the state in its own right. JIMHO Project Doors mentors other Drop-In Centers all around the State of Michigan.

The decisions that you the Board Members make are monumental, not just for the Tri-County, but for the whole state.

From my vantage point, there is little funding for mental health consumer advocacy in our state.

National Alliance on Mental Illness Lansing

is completely run by volunteers. I feel I am

the only one representing the consumers as a

consumer at recent city meetings.

I spoke at the Neighborhoods and Public

Safety Transition Meeting organized by

Mayor-Elect Andy Schor on the importance

of connecting with mental health services

and consumers in our community through

Mental Health First-Aid USA Training for

Public Safety Workers and Open Forums

with needy consumers at Justice in Mental

Health Organization.

I spoke on the importance of these mental health services in lowering crime.

A Neighborhoods and Public Safety Transition Committee Member, L.S., was the only person to address mental health needs (besides me) when she mentioned a JIMHO need.

I spoke at the Lansing Town Hall Meeting as well, organized by Mayor-Elect Andy Schor. I went into more detail about my vantage point.

Police go through a lot of diversity training and seem to show respect to consumers, but the Fire Department and paramedics seem to be lacking and overburdened.

We see a high traffic of police and fire at JIMHO on a regular basis.

It is important for police and fire and paramedics to take the time to meet with consumers and learn their perspectives.

It is a mutual learning opportunity. The police brought four officers to an open forum I organized. I believe the Fire Department needs to make this happen.

This is my view as an active citizen and mental health consumer who has been hospitalized maybe 30 times in my life.

We are making progress and I thank you for your work, but we need your help to equip us to advocate mental health to our city, state, and national leaders.

Lansing, Capital of Michigan is a model to our state.

Let's move forward accordingly.

Thank you,

Daniel K. Arnold

Mental Health Therapy Through Public

Comment

By Daniel K. Arnold

Chapter 5 – Speech #3

August 20, 2018

Consumer Empowerment

What makes us tick and keep fighting the
good fight?

What prevents us from throwing in the
towel?

What makes us become transparent about
our weaknesses so that we may receive the
help that we need?

I have been diagnosed ADHD, Bipolar,
Schizoaffective, Schizophrenic.

My life has meaning and I believe myself to possess diverse super powers—strengths and weaknesses like a comic book character.

I am alive because even as a super hero I realize I need to seek help at times.

How do we reach super heroes?

We must engage their respect before they face moments of catastrophe.

Respect is earned by valuing the contribution of the consumer.

We must teach every super hero that they have something to offer and provide opportunities for them to apply those talents.

I serve on two consumer advisory councils that provide stepping stones for consumers to busy themselves, be productive, and be empathetic.

We the Consumers have something to bring to the table.

I have written books like, The Super Hero Manual that are important to share with the community to have the consumer voice heard.

I believe one of the most crucial aspects to helping super heroes function is to give them opportunities for a structured, productive schedule.

We may be disabled from traditional work, but we still have an innate desire to be productive.

Continue programs like Charter House Clubhouse, art venues, and Writing Club (continue funding).

Encourage the consumer to develop a regular productive schedule.

Some of us have burned many bridges and it becomes difficult to find work.

Encourage this type of super hero to be an entrepreneur.

My gig is to pass out literature in the park, Monday through Friday from about 8-4.

This daily schedule is meaningful to me and those around me. Encourage us to take the time to rest at least one day a week.

We are sensitive.

We are gifted.

We are super heroes.

Thanks for listening!

Mental Health Therapy Through Public

Comment

By Daniel K. Arnold

Chapter 6 – Speech #4

November 30th, 2018

Dear Friends of CMH,

I wish to address a pressing issue in health care today-- Recipient Rights. Having served on the Recipient Rights Consumer Advisory Council for CMHA-CEI and the Midstate Health Network Regional Consumer Advisory Council, I have come to conclusion that (as posted by MDHHS), "Recipient Rights is everybody's business."

Rest assured that CMHA-CEI has many safeguards in place to make sure that mental health consumers are treated with dignity. At the baseline, complaints can be filed with Customer Service to improve quality.

Particularly for violations involving neglect
or abuse, Recipient Rights is in place across
the board-- Crisis Services, JIMHO Drop-In,
Bridges Crisis Unit-- all services under the
CEI umbrella.

Lastly, a process is in place through Access
to file grievances.

We pride ourselves as an agency that
respects consumer rights. Kudos to you all.
Thank You!

As a fellow consumer advocate, I know I
have learned about the mental health system
for a reason. Hands on, I have learned that
every mental health hospital in the state of

Michigan has a Recipient Rights Office

complete with accessible complaint box.

The ability to give feedback on services

without backlash is what we ensure

consumers at their most vulnerable

moments.

Crisis Intervention Team (CIT), based on an

international model to teach police officers

to respond sensitively to mental health crisis

& Mental Health First-Aid USA based on a

national model to train everyone in mental

health emergency response, have been

making headway to accommodate

consumers in emergencies.

Add to that the oversight of police video

monitoring and we are well on our way to a

culture that respects the dignity of the

mental health consumer-- so it would seem.

I am enlisting the consultation of anyone

who will listen about an untapped area of

mental health rights that must be considered.

Universal health care. This may not be your

department, but please listen...

With the move to merge health care

services-- new venues are arising that

provide mental health services with little

care for Recipient Rights. I want your

advice, anyone who will help me on how to

implement the Recipient Rights Complaint

box in ambulances and general hospitals.

Sparrow Hospital has a new closed wing

similar to Crisis Services with no complaint

box in sight. I have spent time in a regular

hospital bed asking for a complaint form,

but being told I couldn't grieve while in the

hospital.

When I asked for a complaint form in an

ambulance, the response was:

Do you mean a HIPPA complaint form? (He

was unable to hand me any form.)

The right to grieve helps resolve tension. It helps mental health consumers to process and improve mental health.

A grievance process also provides oversight of large hospital systems.

Our nation prides itself on a system of checks and balances to prevent corruption. We have legislative, executive, and judicial branches of the U.S. government.

When I asked East Lansing Police Department for a courtesy ride to Crisis Services, they informed me that they do not send people there anymore, but to Sparrow Main Hospital. If Sparrow has become a first line of mental health, mental health

rights needs to become a priority. I tell you

this to inform you to let you know my

vantage point on mental health services even

when they fall out of you or Midstate Health

Network's jurisdiction.

Anyway you can help please do: Ideas,

professionals, media outlets. Thank you for

your help!

Regards,

Daniel K. Arnold

Mental Health Therapy Through Public

Comment

By Daniel K. Arnold

Chapter 7 – Speech #5

March 22nd, 2019

Hello, My Name is Daniel K. Arnold and I

have been your Non-Compliant mental

health consumer.

I am affiliated with the Worldwide Protest

of the American Psychiatric Association and

specialize in Independent Investigative

Journalism.

My findings for CMHA-CEI are rather

shocking to me. During my appointments,

most staff have treated me with the utmost

dignity and respect.

If I ever have a problem, there are 3

different departments ready to receive

grievances: Customer Service, Recipient

Rights, and Access.

I am very thankful for what you guys do!

You are approachable and I enjoy speaking

my perspective at Board Meetings.

I am an advocate for mental health consumers, the homeless, and ex-offenders. Recently, I have gone deeper into investigative journalism. Every setback and disability has become an asset.

I believe mental health consumers are not sick. We don't have a disease. We are special. See my book:

https://www.amazon.com/Super-Hero-Manual-Daniel-Arnold/dp/1499276419

We are Super Heroes with accentuated strengths and weaknesses. Weaknesses become blind spots and I have discovered

that I need the help of my case manager.

I am speaking to you right now like a peer. I

am empowered. Every voice matters.

Together we can set a tone for Community

Mental Healths around the state of

Michigan.

Life is exciting.

Life is good.

I want to meet with each one of you and

learn your perspectives just as I value

learning the consumers you serve.

All things are possible.

I love being here.

Thank You!

Introduce yourself to me. Have a great day!

Mental Health Therapy Through Public

Comment

By Daniel K. Arnold

Chapter 8 – Speech #6

Life Is Not Over At Disability

By Daniel K. Arnold

May 16th, 2019

(Wearing a Fake Jail Jumpsuit)

This presentation is directed at staff

members to build confidence in their

consumers.

I've had some mental health sickness since 1st Grade. I recall crying in the classroom because I had to face the consequences for putting burrs in a student's winter hat.

When I was in 2nd Grade, my little brother mentioned I needed to see "the cry doctor."

Eventually I would receive the diagnosis of ADHD, followed by Bipolar,

Schizoaffective and Schizophrenic.

In 2006, I began receiving disability money from the government.

I am here to tell you, (and) your consumers that life is not over at disability diagnosis and receiving SSI or SSDI.

Empower them. Speak life. Let them know they are special.

Only recently have I begun to discover that my Higher Power has a great plan for my life.

For years I let the stigma of crazy hit me. I felt debilitated, ashamed until I discovered my voice.

I am a writer. I am spiritual. I follow God. I am a Super Hero. I am an Investigative Journalist.

I have a purpose and in this moment I'm
here to tell you to speak life into your
clients-- especially if they have suicidal
ideology.

Just because paper says we Super Heroes are
disabled does not mean we can't find
meaning.

We can volunteer. We can write articles
from our own unique perspectives. We can
visit and spend quality time with others. We
can take action.

We can discover and report injustice to
make this world a better place.

We are all different and we matter. No one can do the things your client does exactly as she/he does them.

Encourage your clients to pursue their dreams. College scholarships? No problem. It doesn't hurt to try. GED, he's going the distance. He's going for speed.

Anything is possible and because he/she is not tied down, he/she can do whatever he/she wants to do to help society.

You can put on a prison jumpsuit right? In our region there are nature parks and woods. There are opportunities to get a free bicycle. There are special speaking engagements to attend on various topics.

Tell your client you support him or her in aiming for his/her dreams.

As a disabled consumer of mental health services, I have completed my degree at LCC Honors Program and MSU College of Elementary Education.

I achieved this with a misdemeanor. I could not be told no. And I went on through a rocky, crazy life institutionalized numerous times.

I cannot be stopped.

I will not give up.

I am branching out.

I am living life to the fullest writing books,

getting published, advocating through

multiple forms of media and 2 advisory

councils.

I've even presented twice to CMHA

Michigan.

It is possible to live a fulfilling life with

disability. Empower your consumers today.

Mental Health Therapy Through Public

Comment

By Daniel K. Arnold

Chapter 9 – Speech #7

August 22nd, 2019

Hello, I am Daniel K. Arnold. The first day

I set foot on CMH property was

uncomfortable in the Summer of 1999. I

had originally been told to be silent about

mental on social media. I never knew I

would one day thrive. I am thankful for the

Open Meetings Act. As a result, I feel

empowered to get to know City Leaders.

In mental health, things can seem black and

white when we truly live in a grey malleable

society. Like many consumers, I was under

the impression that police officers and CMH

were the enemy. As a young adult, I was

locked up for my involvement in the 1999

MSU Riots. I lost many connections and I

hated my introduction to mental health.

I had soul searching to do and few friends.

With time, law enforcement and mental

health built relationships with me. If I had

one thing to complain about it would be the

high turnover of case managers. These

wonderful social workers have made great

efforts to pour into my lie person-centered

planning and I miss them again and again.

They've all been special to me in their own

way, including my latest to be relocated

Case Manager Melissa Doss.

We need continuity of care at CMH. Work

on this as an agency please.

Today I am here to talk about a great

colleague of mine: D.S. right here beside me

wearing the same shirt and hat as me. She is

a great listener, cares about activism, and is

eager to get involved with mental health as a

consumer like I am.

I recommend her for any opportunity for

peer support or advisory council

involvement. She will not let you down.

Thanks for your time! Let's be a model for

the State.

Mental Health Therapy Through Public

Comment

By Daniel K. Arnold

Chapter 10 – Speech #8

Daniel K. Arnold, D.S.

September 19th, 2019

Board of Directors Meeting CMHA-CEI

Hi My name is Daniel K. Arnold and this is

my research partner, D.S.. Despite our

disabilities, we are eager to be involved and

give back to our community. The Tri-

County Area is a wonderful place to live and

thrive.

Recently, we have been studying the

International and Memphis Model for the

Crisis Intervention Team (CIT). Beyond

wanting to present to future CIT Officers in

law enforcement about our perspectives, D.

and I are eager to write a guide for

consumers in laymen's term called, "The

Citizen's Guide to Crisis Response."

Much energy is put into teaching law

enforcement and mental health professionals

to respond to crisis. It is time to empower consumers, friends, and family to advocate for themselves and others in mental health emergencies.

D.S. is by my side to critique my work, be an advocate and partner with me on this adventure. "We have a voice." We are eager to be involved in our community and make a difference. We find the LPD Chief to be very accessible and knowledgeable. It is great to conversate with this PHD Graduate who attended FBI National Academy. Lansing has great potential.

Recently, LPD has released a new phone app on the Play Store that everyone should look into:

Lansing Police Department Mobile PD. On the app is the opportunity to leave tips on crime, commend officers, and access a very large directory of specific LPD numbers. Please share this app with your mental health community. Some consumers are apprehensive about meeting with the police. This app opens a tip online chat line that allows for pictures, location, and being anonymous.

I am impressed by this accommodation the police provide and I encourage you to familiarize yourself with it to advocate and help consumers.

If any of you have input for the Citizen's Guide--- including Crisis Response and the Grievance Process, please get in touch with us.

Thanks,

Daniel K. Arnold & D.S.

Mental Health Therapy Through Public

Comment

By Daniel K. Arnold

Chapter 11 – Speech #9

Daniel K. Arnold

10/17/2019

CMHA-CEI Board of Directors Meeting

<u>Faith Stigmatized As Psychosis</u>

(This presentation topic is crucial to me and

has been viewed over 550 times on social

media.)

Hello, My name is Daniel K. Arnold. I am an author, presenter, and member of two consumer advisory councils. It has come to my attention that in the Tri-County Area, in psychiatric circles, hearing from God is labeled psychosis. I aim to challenge that paradigm. In my faith, I believe that true communication with the Higher Power involves words of comfort from God.

At the NAMI Lansing Faith and Mental Health Meeting Dr. Abbas made a dangerous statement:

"If you talk to God that is fine, but if God talks to you come talk to me."

This is not the first time I have heard such rhetoric:

In 2018, during an evaluation at Sparrow Main Hospital, a professional wrote a very interesting evaluation of me: "AUDITORY HALLUCINATIONS: PT REPORTS: I TALK TO GOD AND GOD TALKS TO ME."

In January of 2018, I met in the office of a CMHA-CEI psychiatrist shortly before work. The care provider stated:

"The facts about Jesus are largely mythical and your willingness to die for children modeling after Jesus is inappropriate as a mental health consumer. I have the power to commit you to a hospital right now."

We need to be careful to acknowledge the faith of diverse consumers. The Bible says, "Greater love has no man than this that he lay down his life for his friend." (John 15:13)

Why is self-sacrifice and faith celebrated at a Fallen Police Officer Ceremony with Former Lansing Police Chief Yankowski speaking his heart with this Scripture yet in a mental health setting a consumer cannot take a similar stance against human trafficking?

In my faith, I hear from God and I obey Him.

"But the Comforter, which is the Holy Ghost, whom the Father will send in my name, he will teach you all things and bring all things to your remembrance, whatsoever I have spoken unto you." (John 14:26)

Through the Holy Spirit, Jesus is the

Comforter. A popular hymn echoes the

reality of God comforting believers:

"And He walks with me and He talks with

me and He tells me I am His own and the

joy we share as we tarry there none other

has ever known."

Please encourage communication to mental

health consumers that they have the right to

change providers through CMH Access if

they feel their rights are being violated.

Please push for an inclusive environment

that respects the faith of consumers.

And please do not neglect your own personal walk with God when you step into the mental health field.

Thank you.

Best Regards,

Daniel K. Arnold

Mental Health Therapy Through Public

Comment

By Daniel K. Arnold

Chapter 12 – Speech #10

November 21st, 2019

<u>Did You Take Your Medicine?</u>

<u>Finding Balance In A Dehumanized World</u>

By Daniel K. Arnold

LCC Honors Program and MSU Alumnus,

Former Faith Tech Bible School Student

Medication comes in many styles and forms.

Some is needed for immediate survival.

Other types are for health maintenance over

the course of a lifetime.

Everyone seems to diversify their position of 100%, 0%, and in between support for taking prescription drugs. In 8th grade, as a hyperactive student, I found myself being offered a prescription for Ritalin, also known as the drug Methylphenidate. When it came down to it, I had the choice of popping that little stimulant in my family's bathroom.

I remember experiencing an immediate change. All my problems seemed to slip away. I had taken my medicine and any detour from this ideal condition would be credited to missing a dose. I achieved a

transformation of school performance and

behavior, as long as I continued on Ritalin.

I impressed my teachers and received

college scholarships. Any deviance from

optimal behavior would be met with this

question, "Did you take your medicine?"

When I worked in a day care, the Ritalin

Mystique hit my subconscious. Why are the

kids suddenly acting up? It must be because

I didn't take my medicine! Uh oh…

Pandora's Box opened.

In 1999, I had a breakdown in jail as a

consequence of my actions in an East

Lansing Riot.

Besides the trauma of shame, having to

move, being removed from training with the

college team, and being removed for the

time being from Sunday School

Volunteering, now I was in jail. As I fell

apart, the jail nurse informed me that my

Ritalin supply was out.

Over the years there has been some

controversy over this borderline Baby

Crack. Can we rig our kids to behave? At

the day care I worked at, a school-aged kid was having behavioral issues. Over time, his actions somehow improved. He needed encouragement and I told his parent about his wonderful change.

Her Response: "The medication is working."

I was disappointed by the statement. Why cannot we treat our little ones with affirmations for good behavior? Does a medication deserve all the credit for positive actions? There will be moments when children will not be able to cope by taking a prescription.

Years ago I asked a psychiatrist for the wonder drug Ritalin.

Her Response: "I never diagnosed you ADHD. (No.)"

Should we stimulate our kids to get immediate results or should we teach them how to cope?

In this journey, I have taken on many different points of view towards medicine. Physicians and psychiatrists are not always right, but they also not always wrong. Is there a middle-ground position a mental health consumer such as myself can take?

Faith is an important aspect of my health. In my walk with God, I have learned to think for myself, explore the Bible for myself, and come to an independent conclusion regarding mental health treatment.

Lesson #1

Learn all through life. If you do not agree with others, take time to listen to investigate the truth.

I have learned from many different church denominations. I find myself reaching the conclusion that I cannot agree with every well meaning opposing viewpoint at the same time.

Some leaders have told me to take my medicine.

Some have tried to deliver me from demonic oppression.

Some have suggested that I need to be healed and stop needing psychotropic drugs, also known as "pharmakeia."

Many have missed the mark.

Our world has become polarized. Most positions are either considered 100% right or in error based on the indoctrination of polarized special interest groups we belong to.

I have discovered myself as an independent investigative journalist. I desire to take the time to listen to all my fellow humans and my God. Not everything has to be set in stone for me as a Republican Jesus Christ Follower who happens to be a mental health consumer.

At times, others are mistaken. Many times I am wrong. We learn. Today my bestfriend asked me in the car, "Did you take your medication?" He was annoyed by me at that moment. Everyone makes errors. I love him and this statement triggered memory of childhood judgment of me as a human being who is more than a disorder or sickness needing a quick fix.

In 2014, I wrote my first book, "The Super Hero Manual." I have come to the conclusion that I am not sick, but am blessed to have a unique personality—a make-up this world needs. I am a Super Hero with the aliases Mister Energy Plus and Black Bird Ops.

It wasn't long ago that rapper Kanye West came out of the mental health closet: He eloquently said, "I'm not Bipolar. I'm a Super Hero." In society, we two own our personalities and know we are special. We are not a mistake, disorder, or perfect.

After many years of fighting, I have reached the conclusion that a very small dosage of anti-psychotic medication works for me. Theoretically, I ride the wave between psychosis and genius. My point of view is that I own my personality. I go through fluctuations of being down and sad. During these moments, I realize that I will eventually naturally fluctuate back to a heightened sense of well-being. I wait it out. I sleep extra.

Lesson #2:

Communicate with your mental health provider no matter how good or bad you feel.

Over the years I have learned to attend all my appointments being honest with my mental health treatment team. We do not always agree, yet my current psychiatrist has great compassion. She is a mother herself who cares. She says, "I am worried about you leaving your baseline."

I respectfully disagree and my prescription has been changed to just a little anti-psychotic medication anyway.

Every appointment I have results in her saying that I can seek help sooner than my next appointment if the need arises. I have been through many different case managers as CMHA-CEI keeps changing their employees positions. This is difficult, but I enjoy the appointments still.

I have the opportunity to share my adventures and receive friendly valuable feedback. I have gone through many periods on and off medication. I have fallen on my face, but I stand before you right now with dignity.

<u>Lesson #3:</u>

Keep moving forward! Thanks for letting me share.

Mental Health Therapy Through Public

Comment

By Daniel K. Arnold

Chapter 13 – Conclusion

Life is worth living. Therapy is a must to attend. I gather a great deal of support from drop-ins, the leaders I speak to and the Church Body, Life is worth living and exciting as a mental health consumer who has discovered a purpose. Thank you for pouring into my life. I look forwards to the future.

Best Regards,

Daniel

(Find my Journalism Account on Facebook:

Guy Smilie (Lansing, MI)